insight text guide

Fiona Neilson

Look Both Ways

Sarah Watt

First published in 2006, reprinted 2007, 2008, 2009, 2017

Insight Publications Pty Ltd
3/350 Charman Road
Cheltenham VIC 3192
Australia
Tel: +61 3 8571 4950
Fax: +61 3 8571 0257
Email: books@insightpublications.com.au

www.insightpublications.com.au

National Library of Australia Cataloguing-in-Publication data:
Neilson, Fiona Oldroyd, 1971–.
Sarah Watt's Look Both Ways: text guide.
For secondary students.
ISBN 9781921088667.
1. Watt, Sarah. Look Both Ways. I. Title.
791.4372

Cover design: Gisela Beer

Printed in Australia

contents

CHARACTER MAP

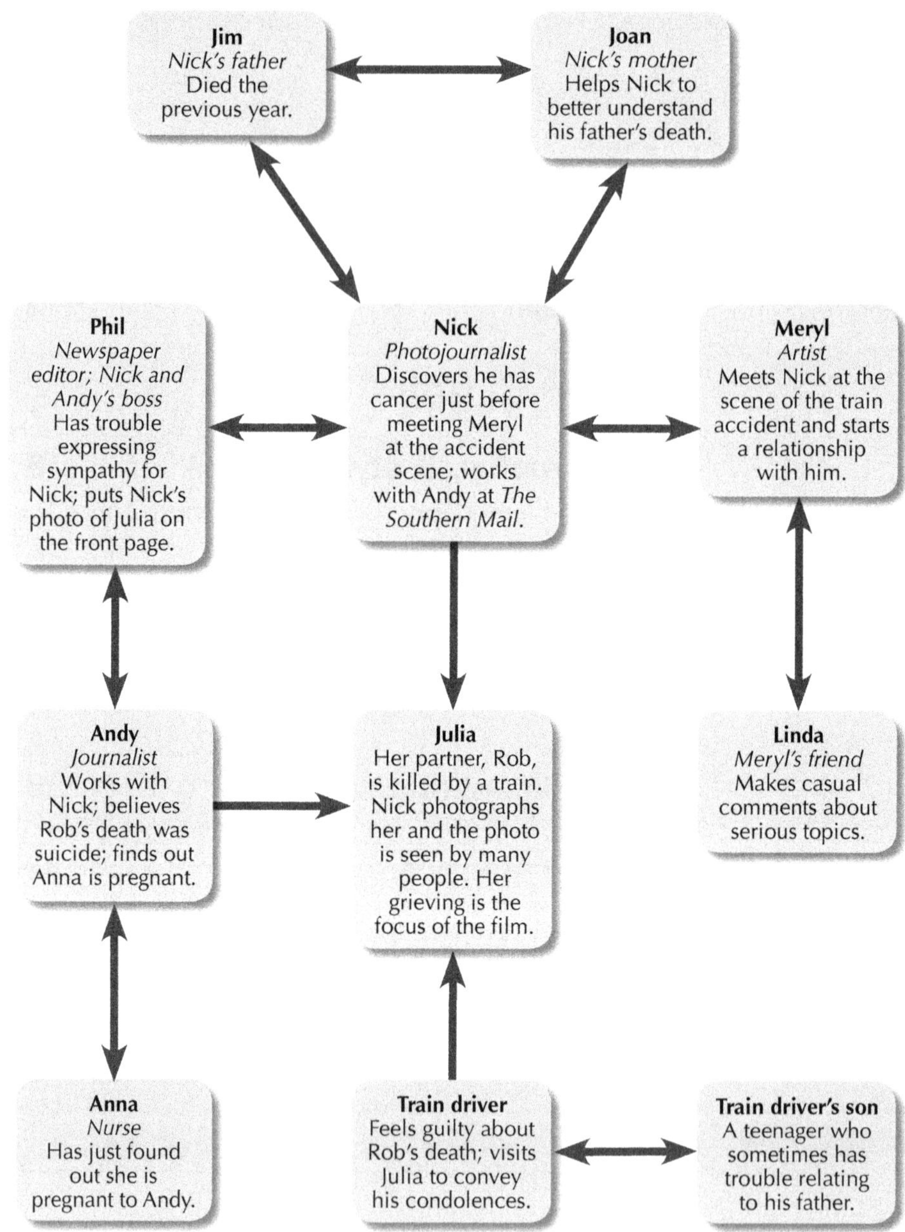

INTRODUCTION

Look Both Ways is a quirky, multi-layered exploration of the different lives being lived over one hot weekend in an Australian city. It occurs in a world criss-crossed by train tracks, in a small urban community made up of an endearing set of characters. Everyone is undergoing their own problems and trying to find their own way of coping with life events; the ways in which these lives intersect and affect one another provides the material for the film.

Originally entitled *Life Story* in the script, *Look Both Ways* raises the issue of what it is to be human in a way that is both humorous and meaningful. The film received much critical acclaim for its ability to tackle the big questions about life and death without being ponderous and dull. Some of the most touching moments of the film are not contained within lengthy dialogue, but rather are conveyed through small gestures and solely visual cues: the clasping of a proffered hand, an ice-cream cone dropped on a driveway, a splash of dirty water over a nearly finished painting. It is these details which stay with the viewer long after the film has finished, reinforcing the fact that ordinary moments have as much place in our lives as the extraordinary ones.

BACKGROUND & CONTEXT

Writer and director Sarah Watt's inclusion of animation sequences and photomontage provides an innovative way of showing what characters are thinking and feeling. The short clips of lone swimmers being crunched by sharks are instantly understandable by Australian viewers, who can identify with Meryl's preoccupations. Similarly, Nick's endless mental picture-show of the causes and progression of his cancer is something that anyone who has ever obsessed about an event in their life can relate to. In another way, the images of menacing stormy seas create a poetic and lyrical visual feel for the film, reminding us that there is more to life than what we see on the surface.

Another film by Sarah Watt, *Living With Happiness* (2001), shows how the themes in *Look Both Ways* developed. This earlier short film is an animation that shows a woman who experiences continual paranoid fears about the potential for disaster in everyday life. Worn down by her constant anxiety, she takes a trip to the beach to relax, only to be swept out to sea by a huge wave and nearly drowning before being saved by a child on a surfboard. As in *Look Both Ways*, it takes a real event of life-threatening significance for the main protagonist to realise that her anxieties have got out of proportion.

Setting

The film is set in an inner city suburb that could be anywhere in Australia. The train disaster occurs in the fictional suburb of Arnow Hill to create a sense in viewers that the events depicted could have happened anywhere in Australia. While *Look Both Ways* was filmed on location in Adelaide, the film's setting is not specifically mentioned, and the newspaper, *The Southern Mail*, does not really exist. Australian viewers will recognise real current affairs and news programs that are imitated in the film. Many of the film's characters live alone or are suffering from a sense of alienation from others and from society in general.

The interrelatedness of all things

The film is permeated by a philosophical stance that promotes the message that all lives are intertwined. Although the film is not specifically affiliated with a particular area of philosophy or religion, its approach can be loosely aligned with a kind of spiritual belief about life that conceives of a unity that holds everything in the universe together.

The film shows a belief that there are universal aspects in nearly all of our experiences, whether they are large or small. Death is something that we are all going to have to face up to at some point and is one of those large experiences that links people together; the film makes this clear through its presentation of different characters' experiences with death. Characters also experience small moments of truth where they see or feel something that a wider audience can relate to. So when Meryl glances at a younger, prettier woman in a bikini at the pool (Segment 5) and the train driver's son tries to make himself as unobtrusive as possible when he returns home at dawn (Segment 4), many viewers will be able to understand and share in their feelings.

This emphasis on common humanity can also be seen in the train scene when Nick and Meryl return from lunch at Nick's mother's place (Segment 10). At one point, Nick looks at the other passengers, seeing them as portraits. He notices all the small details about them that give clues as to who they are: their jewellery, the logos on their clothes, and their activities, such as knitting. This series of close-up head and body shots shows the variety of other people who exist in the world, from a wide range of ages, ethnicities, styles and subcultures.

This is an important point. The film could have emphasised people's differences and sought to show that we are irreconcilably separate from one another, which would have created a bleak, hopeless atmosphere. Instead, the message we take from the film is that we are all linked together through our common fate by virtue of our humanity, which is much more heart-warming and reassuring.

Existentialism

Look Both Ways shares its outlook with the broad tenets of existentialism, a philosophy that asks questions about what it is to be human and what the meaning of life is. Existentialism is concerned with the individual's quest to make meaning and sense out of their life. It often questions the role of death in people's lives, asking what the value is of life when we are all fated to die one day.

One existentialist philosopher, Jean-Paul Sartre, developed a concept of bad faith, which is the state that humans end up in when they do not assume responsibility for their actions and their consequences. Experiencing bad faith involves feeling anxiety and dread. It can be argued that Andy is a classic example of someone who is acting in bad faith in his relationship with Anna, because he is not prepared for much of the film to accept the consequences of his sexual relationship with her. His denial of the situation may account for his bad moods and belligerence. The film suggests that only once someone accepts responsibility for their actions can they relax and find peace with themselves.

Another value espoused by some existentialist philosophers is the notion that life is full of value because it is only lived once, and therefore it should be lived in the moment. Existentialist writers such as Albert Camus argue that if we no longer believe in a god or an afterlife then this can potentially render life meaningless or absurd. Paradoxically, this lack of religious belief can also make life infinitely more precious, because it is only lived once, with no chance of an afterlife. *Look Both Ways* endorses the idea that seizing the moment and acting according to one's authentic impulses is a positive thing. The character of Nick, who pursues a relationship with Meryl when chance throws their paths together again, is shown as being rewarded with a relationship and self-knowledge through this pursuit.

Stages of grief

The psychological conceptualisation of the stages of grief is fundamental to the film's narrative structure and to an understanding of how the characters operate. Meryl actually refers to the seven stages of grief in Segment 7 when Nick asks her whether she is over the shock of the accident and her father's death. The seven stages of grief are:

- shock or disbelief
- denial
- bargaining
- guilt
- anger
- depression
- acceptance and hope

This framework has been developed by psychiatrists to explain the stages that we go through when we lose someone through death, though of course grieving is not restricted to loss through death. Some psychiatrists and psychologists use a five-stage model, while later practitioners work with a seven-stage model. In *Look Both Ways*, the grieving process is related to death, most notably through the character of Julia, who can be seen moving from a state of shock and numbness through anger (when she shoves the dog out of the way as she runs from the house), to a state of acceptance signified when she erects the memorial to Rob, and hope that time will heal her pain when she receives the train driver with a feeling of relief and gladness in Segment 10.

Buddhism

Buddhism is a spiritual and philosophical belief system that could be said to inform the overall philosophical themes of the film. Buddhism aims to end suffering. It promotes an understanding that existence involves suffering, but that this can be overcome or transcended by Buddhist practices that work on purifying the mind. There are Four Noble Truths that are central to Buddhism, which basically move from a recognition that to be alive is to suffer, to a state where adherents manage to find peace. Part of Buddhist teaching involves the Noble Eightfold Path, eight areas that cover practices of ethical conduct and mental discipline that will ultimately lead to the end of suffering. Where the film can be said to share understandings with Buddhism is in its overall stance that life inevitably involves suffering. *Look Both Ways* does not attempt to present life as being easy and pain-free; rather, it shows the awkwardness, discomfort and hurt that people experience on a daily basis, and it always characterises these as a necessary part of existence.

Fate

The idea of fate is referred to regularly throughout the film. Fate is a power that predetermines events. It refers to what is meant to happen, to a fixed pathway or allocated 'lot in life', as though both general and personal destiny had already been decided upon in the larger order of things. A belief in fate presupposes that there is a fixed order in the universe. This idea that fate determines what happens to us is both endorsed and critiqued in the film. See the Themes, ideas & values section and the Different interpretations section for further discussion of ideas about fate in the film.

Arnow Hill disaster as the context for the story

Throughout the film, the Arnow Hill disaster forms a backdrop for the microcosm of life that we witness among the dozen or so characters affected by Rob's death. The film uses this context of a fictional train disaster as the setting for its exploration of how a local accident affects the lives of a small group of people. Although the Arnow Hill rail disaster is a fictional event in the film, we can all relate to the phenomenon of a disaster that is continually discussed and analysed on the television news. Similar events such as the Bali bombings, September 11, the Boxing Day tsunami and the London bombings are all too familiar for contemporary viewers.

Despite our openness to being touched by the suffering of other people, ultimately our personal tragedies can take on as much importance to us as the largest disasters. When people are experiencing their own personal sorrows, it can be very hard for them to put their suffering into perspective.

* * *

In a case of life cruelly imitating art, Sarah Watt was diagnosed with breast cancer while *Look Both Ways* was in post-production. Her husband, William McInnes, who plays Nick in the film and who is also a published writer, has written about her experience with cancer.

Sarah Watt made one more feature film, *My Year Without Sex* (2009), which also deals with the experience of suffering from a life-threatening illness. She died in November 2011.

GENRE, STRUCTURE & STYLE

Genre

Writer/director Sarah Watt describes the film as a romantic comedy. This categorisation may seem a little off-centre, seeing as the film focuses on death. However, it is at the same time about how people pull their lives back together after experiencing the death of loved ones. The story of Meryl and Nick, and also the parallel one of Andy and Anna, shows romance springing from unlikely soil. There is also much black humour, mainly deriving from the incongruous juxtaposition of Meryl's bleak visions of self-destruction with the banal events of everyday life.

Look Both Ways is also a realistic film that does not seek to idealise or glamorise grief nor portray it in an unremittingly serious manner. It is willing to show events of minor significance alongside ones of much greater import. In this respect it is also modest, because it does not make any grandiose, self-important claims to being a definitive portrayal of loss and coping.

Structure

The structure consists of a series of eleven successive episodes that follow a chronological sequence, with some flashbacks and flashforwards. Within this overall chronological sequence are a cluster of intersecting stories that the film moves between, showing each new episode of the sub-stories in sequence. There are several points in the film when the sub-stories are all shown in turn, such as the Saturday night sequence in Segment 8 where we are shown the characters of Julia, Phil and Anna and what they are doing at the same time as the major characters Nick, Meryl and Andy.

There is an element of mystery in that the train driver is not clearly identifiable until the end of the film. When he reveals his identity to Julia, the reason for his inclusion in the earlier scenes becomes clear, and the viewer is able to grasp their significance in retrospect.

Key point

Consider how editing works to shape the narrative and influence our understanding of events. In the script and during filming, the scene where Julia builds her memorial (Segment 10) initially followed the one where she is upset over seeing herself on the first page of the paper (Segment 7). However, during the editing process, this scene was moved to later in the film. The effect of this change is to make it look as though Julia's construction of the memorial has sparked off an acceptance by the other characters of their grief.

The use of flashbacks

Nick's remembering of the end of his father's life shows that only now that he too is suffering from an illness can he understand what his father was experiencing. There is a sense that he is gaining a new understanding of his father's life when his mind returns to these events now. He sees certain events as significant where he previously did not think about them much, or had repressed them.

Style

The film uses a variety of communication modes to convey its messages, and one of its themes is that there are many such modes through which humans communicate. This is shown most obviously through the juxtaposition of visual art with spoken language. The different types of visual art used are static image, photomontage, animation, paintings and drawings. They are used alongside the standard film shots to complement the main narrative. They function to illustrate things in another way – sometimes, emotions and thoughts can be evoked with much more clarity through several pictures than through words.

Q Consider the final photomontage that shows a multitude of life events whirring past, evoking the future for Nick, Meryl and their circle of friends and family. Do you think this is more effective than, say, a voice-over that describes their future life together? Why?

Key point

Nick, in particular, uses Meryl's paintings as clues to her feelings and personality, and this is symbolised by his use of her discarded painting as a 'way into' her personal space.

Visual art is also used to illustrate subtexts. For example, Nick sees that Andy is working himself up so much that he runs the risk of an aneurysm.

The film's style shows each character or set of characters very rapidly at times, indicating that they are all linked in the same moment. The film uses these techniques to show that their lives take place concurrently.

Most of the film is presented from an objective point of view. This enables us to see what characters are doing and provides us with an overview from a central point. At times, however, this point of view shifts to perceptually and mentally subjective ones. We are given frequent perceptual points of view from Nick's perspective, such as when he has flashbacks to his father's illness. In these scenes, we see Nick's father, Jim, through Nick's eyes, and we hear his voice as it blocks out all external sound for Nick. A good example is in the train scene after lunch at his mother's place (Segment 10).

Mentally subjective viewpoints are shown from both Nick's and Meryl's perspectives in the form of the animations and photomontages that they each 'see', and that we are privy to.

The film style is not heavily stylised or cinematic. Rather, it seeks to paint a naturalistic picture of the story and allow the ordinary aspects of the lives of the protagonists to be seen. There are many shots of interiors of houses that show the habitats of the different characters. This helps us to become familiar with the characters, assisting us to move into their worlds and better understand them.

Scene dividers: flying birds

The brief shots of birds flying serve to create a break between scenes, providing a brief moment in which to reflect and move outside of the immediate story until the next scene commences. Note that the sound of the birds' wings is the last sound heard in the film, at the end of the photomontage, suggesting that the characters' lives 'take off' and move ahead into the future. The sound bite reinforces the impression of life running on ahead of us, created by the increasingly rapid visual imagery.

Q Can you think of any other ideas that the shots of birds conjure up?

Symbolism: train tracks

Train tracks feature throughout the film, from being the site of both Rob's death and the Arnow Hill disaster to being an at times discomforting visual reminder of the remorseless nature of machinery. Usually when we see train tracks, we assume that trains will stay on them. However, both Arnow Hill and one of Meryl's early animated visions show that trains do leave their tracks. In this way they provide a metaphor for life: it can stay on the tracks or it can derail. We may have an expectation that our lives will follow a certain predetermined and well-marked path; however, this expectation can be suddenly 'derailed' through unexpected happenings and tragedies.

Symbolism: the heatwave

The heatwave is a stylistic device that symbolises emotions being withheld and the characters' emotional desolation. Several characters have significant events happen to them at the start of the weekend: Julia's partner is killed by the train, Meryl's father dies, Nick finds out that he has cancer and Andy finds out that Anna is pregnant. All of these events create a state of tension for the characters involved. When the rain finally comes on Sunday, so does release. This is reinforced by the fact that many of the characters cry at the same time as the storm finally breaks.

SCENE-BY-SCENE ANALYSIS

Segment 1: 'A bad prognosis'

Summary: *Friday afternoon – Meryl visits her mother's home at the time of the funeral; Meryl returns home; Nick learns that he has cancer and then informs his boss.*

A family death: The theme of death is introduced by both the flowers and sympathy cards received after Meryl's father's death, and by the television news coverage of the train accident at Arnow Hill. We also learn of the hot weather in store for the weekend.

Meryl's return: Meryl returns home on the train on Friday after the funeral. Shots of trains from different angles contrast the small size of humans with these huge machines, and the loud train noises on the soundtrack emphasise the danger that they embody.

Meryl sees Rob in the bushes, imagining at first that he is a mugger before realising that he is just a man playing with his dog. The final shot shows birds wheeling in the sky, a repeated motif in the film.

Key point

The animations of train and car crashes and violent death that are interspersed with the main narrative present Meryl's view of the world, which is particularly dark.

Nick learns of his cancer: Nick, a photojournalist, discusses x-rays of his torso with a doctor who has just told him he has cancer. This information puts Nick in limbo for the rest of the day and over the weekend.

Key scene

A photomontage that approximates moving footage shows an edited movie version of Nick's life so far with its major events, indicating Nick's reflections on mortality.

The newspaper office: The workplace scene at *The Southern Mail* newspaper introduces Nick, his boss Phil, the newspaper editor, and his co-worker, Andy, a journalist. Phil is uncomfortable to hear of Nick's cancer and unsure how to react appropriately, blurting out a silly joke. The shot of Nick leaving Phil's office is a slow edit, showing his whole work environment and conveying to the viewer a sense of who Nick is. Andy shows his humorous side when he answers the phone for Arts Diary in a camp voice. The scene also introduces Andy's interest in male suicide.

Q What do we learn about Nick and Meryl as characters through the use of the animations and photomontage?

Segment 2: 'An accidental meeting'

Summary: *Friday afternoon and evening – Rob has been killed by a train; Nick and Andy record the incident for the newspaper; Anna tells Andy that she is pregnant.*

The train accident: Rob has been killed by a freight train. A slow edit shows the accident scene in its entirety, creating a *mise en scène* of the paramedics, police, journalists, train driver and witness (Meryl). Andy asks Meryl questions, suggesting that it was suicide. Meryl 'sees' another train leave the rails and plough into all of them. When the dead man's partner, Julia, arrives, Nick instinctively raises his camera and photographs her; the freeze frames of her reaction are interspersed with the film and show her dawning realisation of Rob's death.

Key point

The photo of Julia dropping her shopping is an iconic shot that is repeated throughout the film.

Nick and Meryl leave the scene at the same time. They make awkward conversation, discussing death and then wider issues of fate. Nick is stunned when Meryl appears to read his mind, saying 'Cancer' out of the blue. She is in fact talking about her star sign, but it sets up a connection between them.

Anna reveals her pregnancy: Anna, Andy's ex-girlfriend, confronts him with her pregnancy when he returns home from the accident. An uncomfortable scene follows inside the flat. The subdued lighting focuses our attention on the interplay between the characters and on their expressions, and reinforces the sombre tone. Andy is not very forthcoming: he listens but does not say much. Some of what he says is provocative, such as when he asks her whether he is the father of the baby, and whether she has fallen pregnant on purpose. Neither of them is prepared to take decisive action or responsibility for the matter.

Q Describe the mood of the accident scene. Does it appear as a tragic event, or as something that has happened on an ordinary day?

Segment 3: 'Tragedy, despair, grief & art'

Summary: *Friday night – various characters, each with their own story and personal preoccupations, unwind after the day's events: Meryl starts to paint for a Monday deadline; Nick reviews his photos and absorbs his cancer news; Phil puts Nick's photo on the front page of the Saturday paper.*

Meryl starts to paint: Meryl returns to her warehouse studio and we learn that she is an artist/illustrator who has a deadline on Monday. She starts to paint and talks to her sister on the phone about their father's funeral and her dissatisfaction with her life. The animation of sharks encircling a woman swimmer shows that she feels vulnerable and overwhelmed.

Key point

The music commences before the scene in Meryl's studio is finished, linking it to the following ones through a sound bridge that continues until the very end of the scene. This shows how these people's lives are starting to connect.

The other characters work through their personal issues:

- Nick is at home, reviewing his photos of the accident on his laptop, drinking whisky and looking despairing. His photos of death and destruction show that death is on his mind.
- At dusk, Julia watches the trains, alone in her backyard.
- The Arnow Hill train accident is on the television when the train driver returns home. The bigger tragedy of the disaster is happening at the same time as the more personal one of Rob's death.
- Andy is working at his suicide theory, writing an article about Rob's death.
- Anna is at home watching news of the Arnow Hill accident.
- Phil is at work when he receives Nick's emailed photo of Julia.
- Meryl is making a big painting on the floor, painting vigorously as she lets the pent-up tension of the day out through physical movement and artistic creation.
- A newspaper press is printing the Saturday edition of *The Southern Mail* and we see that Nick's picture of Julia is on the cover. The music stops.

Q What mood does the music create: serious, melancholy, light?

Segment 4: 'The news report'

Summary: *Saturday morning – the characters work through the train accident and their own issues: the train driver is still upset by the accident; Andy gets cross with Phil about the photo; Nick wakes up with a hangover and has flashbacks of his father's death.*

The train driver is still upset: The train driver breaks down crying after his son brings in the newspaper. The shots of the train driver and his son are taken from outside the room to keep the viewer remote from the driver's grief. This contrasts with the intimacy created in the next scene with Phil's family.

Phil shows his distance from family life: Phil and his family are having a typically busy morning. Both the Arnow Hill train disaster and Rob's death feature on the front page of the newspaper. Phil forgets that it is his daughter Jasmine's birthday the next day, showing that he is distanced from his family, probably by his work.

Andy berates Phil: Andy calls Phil to complain about the prominent position occupied by Nick's photo. Andy refuses to accept that Rob's death was an accident.

Nick wakes up to the fact of his cancer: Nick has fallen asleep on printouts about cancer. An animation of cancer cells growing into tumours shows what is going through Nick's mind and what his anxieties are. In the shower Nick feels his body numbly, realising the significance of his disease. While showering, Nick experiences a montage showing cancer-related imagery, including media articles about cancer and photos of his exposure to potential carcinogens. This scene emphasises his preoccupation with the disease. Nick also has flashbacks of his father, Jim, in his final months, sparked by the coffee cup.

Key point

Many of the images that Nick relives from his own life are photos. This points to the constructed nature of memory, and to the fact that we all have a perspective through which we view life. For example, Meryl's perspective represents events through drawings and paintings as opposed to the photos that Nick experiences.

Nick jogs down the street and sees his photo on the paper. Out the front of Julia's house, a car from a funeral director pulls up as Nick watches. The funeral industry has started its task of dealing with Rob's death.

Julia goes through the motions: Inside, Julia is looking at coffin choices in a funeral brochure. Shots taken from outside the room and through the window make her look alone and reinforce the idea that we are observers, getting a glimpse of Julia's grief but not being able to enter into it with her.

Q What information does the interaction between the train driver and his son tell us about their relationship?

Segment 5: 'Signs of death'

Summary: *Saturday morning – Meryl and Nick meet again outside Meryl's studio; Nick sees death everywhere; Linda and Meryl go to the pool for relief from the heat.*

Meryl sees death everywhere: Meryl is reading the paper with the photo of Julia on the front. This photo is the thread drawing many of these characters' different lives together. Meryl sees death everywhere in the newspaper; an animation of Meryl's windows imploding and the floor cracking open beneath her feet depicts her sense of dread. This annoys her so she crushes up the paper angrily and takes it out to the recycling bin, where Nick happens to be passing.

Nick and Meryl have another awkward conversation: Meryl appears embarrassed to be seen in her pyjamas, and Nick tries to apologise for his and Andy's behaviour the previous day. Nick notices her discarded painting and takes it.

Key point

Meryl's painting is the connection that brings Nick back to her, while Nick's photo is arguably the reason why they meet again (she is throwing out that paper when he passes). They connect through images. Both use images for work and to communicate.

Nick sees death everywhere: Down the street, Nick sees everyday occurrences as strange and deathly. A hearse drives past, the butcher's shop appears gruesome and a sick boy in a wheelchair appears ghoulish to Nick until the boy suddenly smiles sweetly.

Key point

Note how the film slows down and the sound is muffled while the sick child passes, emphasising Nick's realisation that death is happening around him. It may be that the fact of his cancer is sinking in.

Death in the water: Linda arrives. Her medical test result mix-up emphasises the theme that good and bad things are happening around us all the time and that tragedies can unfold in very ordinary surroundings. At the pool, Meryl projects her paranoid fears of death onto Maddy, who is floating face down in the water. When Meryl first enters the water, she appears to be peaceful, and we see a calm animation of Meryl swimming over a beautiful coral reef. However, in the next animation scene, she imagines that she is being eaten by a shark.

Segment 6: 'Godless'

Summary: *Saturday midday – Nick and Andy are playing in a cricket match and having a philosophical conversation; Anna is constantly reminded of her pregnancy; Phil attempts to discuss Nick's cancer with him again.*

While they wait their turns to bat at the cricket game, Andy is antagonistic towards Nick for having had his photo put on the front page, and makes a comment about how Nick may as well die now. This is ironic for the viewers, who know of Nick's cancer.

Religious beliefs: Nick 'sees' animations of cancer from smoking and melanomas. He has a series of flashbacks to his father making comments about religion. When Nick subsequently asks Andy if he believes in God, Andy is dismissive. Nick 'sees' Andy's aneurism as Andy carries on about religion in his usual angry, disdainful way. Andy then asks Nick if he has ever got anyone pregnant, indicating his preoccupations.

Anna is asked whether she has any children: In the children's hospital's emergency ward, Anna, who works as a nurse, deals with sick children. It seems to Anna that everyone is interested in her reproductive state, which provides a constant reminder of her predicament.

Back at the cricket, Phil makes awkward conversation with Nick, displaying a stereotypical understanding of cancer sufferers, and implying that he put the photo on the front page to make Nick feel better. Nick plays badly, suggesting that he is distracted by other things.

Segment 7: 'Death is everywhere'

Summary: *Saturday afternoon and early evening – some of the characters move further into their situations: Julia becomes upset over the newspaper photo; the train driver and his son cannot communicate; Nick and Meryl both realise they have been seeing death everywhere.*

Rituals of mourning: Meryl makes a small memorial out of found objects next to the accident site. A song starts to play and continues through the following scenes, creating a sweet, sad and reflective mood. The scene cuts to Julia trying to write a death notice but giving up, throwing down her pen in frustration. She is upset when she sees the display of her grief on the newspaper cover.

Tragedy and happiness exist side-by-side: The train driver and his son are still not communicating very well. Meanwhile, Miriam is decorating a birthday cake. Phil looks pleased – he is giving up smoking. Their happy moment contrasts with the tragedy that the train driver's family is working through.

Temporary relief from the heat: Anna walks under the sprinkler. She takes pleasure in the relief from the heat that this gives her; it is still blazingly hot. Cut to the train, shot from two very close-up angles, which fills the screen with its noise and movement and stops the relaxed, dreamy mood of the scene instantly.

Andy and Cathy's relationship: Andy is on the train when Cathy (his ex-wife) calls him. She is cross about his article as she thinks it is about them.

Meryl and Nick move closer: Nick decides to visit Meryl when he sees her painting on his fridge. His arrival startles her. They are awkward together, standing apart in one shot, which emphasises their separation. Both speak rather stiltedly until they find out that they are both interested in death. Meryl is self-conscious about Nick being there: she hides her paintings and underwear, and is self-aware when she mentions sex.

Key point

The animations in this scene continue to reveal the characters' underlying preoccupations: Meryl's vision of Nick as an intruder shows her fear not only of strangers, but perhaps also of intimacy. The killer whale animation shows that Meryl is thinking about death at the same time as Nick, who raises the subject immediately afterwards.

Q Why is Julia upset to see her photo in the newspaper?

Segment 8: 'Synchronicities'

Summary: *Saturday night – A number of characters are in reflective moods in this scene: Anna thinks about her pregnancy and options, and Andy wants to speak to Anna. Nick and Meryl sleep together.*

Anna and Andy are still working things out: Anna is at home, tired, looking at the pregnancy options brochure. Andy is watching *Macbeth*, the play he is meant to review for Arts Diary, though he leaves before the end. Cut to Anna's house, where Rob's death has become the subject of other people's dinner party conversations. Andy calls Anna and there are lots of silences as neither wants to take a decisive step towards the other. Andy's comment to the barman, 'Why do people have sex?', leads directly into the next scene in an amusing way.

Meryl and Nick: In bed with Nick, Meryl 'sees' animations of pregnancy and AIDS, showing her anxieties yet again. A jaunty song plays. Nick 'sees' animations of cancer cells and of the relationship of the sex act to cancer. There is a shot of their groins pressing together, which looks very biological and unsexy. The noise of their kissing continues over the top of the film of cells multiplying, while the film shows sperm racing past the cancer tumour. In the end, Meryl 'sees' a peaceful image of herself floating in water, her face in the sunlight. Nick's cancer cells cease to divide and grow and start to recede. Her image transposes onto the film of his cancer cells; both have found peace together.

Time to reflect: Andy is watching television at home, drinking and eating takeaway. The news is either disastrous, sordid or banal. Sick of television, Andy puts some sad, reflective music on. This music continues to the end of the scene, linking the characters' emotional states. Anna is sitting in her backyard alone while the others laugh indoors.

Three solitary characters look at the moon and reflect on their lives:

- Phil looks at the washing on the line and reflects on his family.
- Julia grieves in the backyard.
- The train driver, who still looks upset and despondent, is troubled by his conscience.

Nick gets up, leaving Meryl in bed asleep. He sees her shark painting and another one where she is sitting alone with her head bowed, suggesting that he is starting to understand who she is. Nick appears to be reading these images for information about Meryl, which is what we as viewers do. Nick leaves and on the street sees a drunk kid, looking at the moon. Meryl awakens and birds scatter at dawn.

Segment 9: 'Family matters'

Summary: *Sunday morning – Nick visits Meryl and invites her to his mother's for lunch; Andy looks after his children for the afternoon.*

A bad start to the day: Andy shows his grouchy side again when he argues with the shopkeeper over an increase in prices and shouts 'Shut up!' at a choir inside a church. The church music segues into the next shot, of Anna watching a gospel church service on television.

Death of Nick's father: In bed, Nick has flashbacks of Jim on the beach, discussing his sickness and treatment. Nick returns hesitantly to Meryl's flat. They have an awkward conversation talking about when her dad died, and then about his father's death. The toast burns because Meryl does not want to interrupt what Nick is saying. Nick tries but fails to tell Meryl about his cancer, then invites her to lunch at his mum's.

Andy's children: Andy picks up his children, Oliver and Maddy, for the afternoon. Their mother, Cathy, appears overcautious with her endless instructions and her Volvo. She obviously has little confidence in Andy's ability to look after the children as well as she would like. He takes the kids to an art exhibition in the hope that they will learn something; however, they are not very willing participants.

Segment 10: 'Connectivity'

Summary: *Sunday lunch and afternoon – Nick and his mother discuss the death of Nick's father; Julia builds a memorial; Andy and Anna have an argument; Meryl and Nick also have an argument; Andy and Nick end up at the train accident site; the rain starts.*

Key scenes

These scenes brings events to a climax for the main characters, and show them tackling the problems that have been building up over the weekend. The scenes show them reaching catharses, where they let go of pent up emotion and start to feel relief from their anxiety and worries.

Understanding his father's death: At Nick's mother's place, where Nick and Meryl have gone for lunch, Nick revisits his father's death. He experiences this both through flashbacks and through conversation with his mother, Joan. Nick gets heated about his father's cancer and his approach to it, but Joan argues that what matters is how life is lived, and that someone's death is not the sum of their life. Nick's mother is unaware that he is thinking a lot about his father's death in relation to his own diagnosis of cancer.

Julia's memorial: Once Julia starts to find a way through her grief, other people also start to find a way through the impasses in their relationships. When Julia sees Meryl's memorial, she becomes very upset and destroys it, then returns home and builds her own memorial with her dead partner's tools. Instead of following the socially prescribed rituals of choosing coffins and writing death notices, Julia is making her own personal ritual. The film represents this as a turning point for Julia. This is shown in two ways:

- The music introduces a more upbeat tone, as though something is getting into motion.
- The image of Julia putting Rob's gloves on is powerful, as it shows that she is getting closer to him through this act.

Family scenes: The train driver's son brings a beer to his father in the garden in a conciliatory gesture. He has also dressed conservatively, trading his gothic clothes for a neat shirt and pants. The song lyrics seem to articulate what the characters cannot: 'it hurts so bad'. Andy and his kids are enjoying themselves, relaxed at last. At Jasmine's party, Phil watches the children playing and looks happy.

Nick is absorbed in thoughts of his father: On the train with Meryl, Nick misses the stop. Flashbacks show Nick's father when very ill, and how helpless Nick felt to help.

Anna confronts Andy: When Andy returns home with the children, Anna is waiting and raises the issue of the baby again. She stresses that this is as much Andy's responsibility as hers and that it was not planned, that 'things just happen'. Andy walks past Julia's house; he looks as though he is reflecting on Rob's death, and showing sensitivity for the first time in the film.

Nick tells Meryl he doesn't want to start anything: Walking through the park, Nick tells Meryl he can't start a relationship with her. Remember that at this stage he still hasn't told Meryl he's got cancer. Meryl is hurt; she makes many angry statements. She chastises herself for being too polite, and all her fears and loneliness well up. Then Nick finally tells her about his diagnosis. She asks, 'You're dumping me because you've got cancer? Shouldn't I be dumping you if you've got cancer?' She runs off, overwhelmed by the situation, narrowly avoiding being hit by a car.

Andy and Nick reach their personal crisis points: Andy returns to the train tracks, very upset. He almost lets himself get run over by a train. Nick, who has been racing the train, sees the whole incident. Standing next to Julia's memorial, Nick reveals he has cancer, a fact that Andy finds hard to take in.

Q Why does Julia destroy Meryl's memorial?

Q How does music function in the final scene between Andy and Nick?

Segment 11: 'Life – it's meant to be'

Summary: *Sunday afternoon – Many characters' situations are resolved as the rain falls: Julia meets the train driver; Meryl and Nick reconcile; Andy visits Anna; we get a glimpse of their future lives.*

The rain signifies release in this segment as many of the characters cry and find relief from their situations. Nick, Meryl and Anna cry as they come to terms with their situations.

A reconciliation: The train driver visits Julia with a card (painted by Meryl) to express his sorrow. For some viewers, this will be the point at which they realise the connection between these two characters. Julia clasps his hand, and they both speak their only lines of the film. This represents a further step in the process of healing.

Relief: Both Andy and Meryl, in separate scenes, start to laugh at their situations, showing that they are letting go of their anxieties and frustrations. Phil enjoys his daughter's birthday, while Joan smiles at the good news when a child is found alive in the train wreck. The rain has stopped; Nick and Meryl meet again and kiss.

The future: A montage of photos rolls past, like a film, showing future events in the characters' lives. It shows Nick having treatment for cancer, Nick and Meryl's future travels, Meryl at an exhibition of her work and Andy with a baby. It shows the myriad of moments, both happy and sad, that make up people's lives. Notice that the sound of birds flapping comes at the end of the montage, reinforcing this idea that lives are taking off, continuing beyond the end of this film. The calypso-style music that plays over the credits, with its lyrics 'never ever worry', creates an upbeat, happy tone.

CHARACTERS & RELATIONSHIPS

Meryl

Key quotes

'Maybe it was meant to be .... Maybe the right thing happens.' (Segment 2)

'I suppose everyone has to witness something ghastly one day.' (Segment 5)

'My dad died two weeks ago. Why isn't my picture on front of the paper? Why isn't everybody who loses somebody on the front bloody page?' (Segment 10)

'The seven stages of grief. What's the point in knowing where you're up to if you've still got to go through it anyway?' (Segment 7)

Meryl is an artist who has a deadline – providing illustrations for a book by Monday. She has just returned home from her father's funeral, and our introduction to her occurs in this context of death. Meryl is in shock, and her visions of violent death, in the form of animations, testify to her preoccupation with the theme of death. She has many fears and anxieties working on different levels. Her fears of death, as shown in the animations, are one sort; she is also afraid of being alone, as she says herself during her argument with Nick. These anxieties may come in part from extreme sensitivity and a lack of a thick skin that would protect her from life events better; they may also come from a passive attitude towards the world that means that she accepts whatever fate hands to her rather than trying to exert influence on her circumstances.

Meryl is one of the most reflective characters in the film, often voicing questions about the role of fate that link into some of the major themes. When she says, 'Maybe it was meant to be' about Rob's death, she then has the self-awareness to realise that her comment could be seen as flippant.

For much of the film, Meryl accepts the events that happen to her. It is only when she feels that her relationship with Nick is in danger that she speaks out and questions what's happening to her.

She emphasises the universality of suffering when she asks why her picture was not on the front page. In saying this, she appears to crave some acknowledgement of her individual suffering. She is making the point that most of the world's suffering is overlooked or ignored, whereas other suffering is endlessly promoted through the media.

Key point

Meryl's argument with Nick represents a crisis point for her, when all her fears and anxieties come to a head. She finally speaks her fears out loud. She asks Nick, 'What if it is shallow and stupid to be lonely and to want somebody to like you?' (Segment 10). This marks a change because up until this point in the film Meryl has only experienced her sense of vulnerability in the form of her animations. She finds this experience, as well as the revelation of Nick's diagnosis with cancer, so overwhelming that she has to run away afterwards, instead of staying and working it through further with Nick.

It is significant that for much of the film Meryl imagines terrible things happening to her, and that nothing happens. Yet when something threatening does happen to her, when she falls in front of the speeding car, she does not have time to project her paranoid fears onto the incident. She is too busy living the moment to philosophise about it. This suggests that many of her fears are unfounded and serve no purpose because they do not bear any relation to real life. It also suggests that for much of the film she has been living in her thoughts rather than in the moment.

Nick

Key quotes

'Do you believe in God?' (Segment 6)

'Poverty, war, natural disaster ... then back to the minibar.' (Segment 7)

'I've been seeing death everywhere this weekend ... I just look at people and I see them dying.' (Segment 7)

'There's always this stuff in the paper about a brave-battle-with-cancer but then you're also supposed to accept it and have a nice everybody-gather-round-and-hug-each-other death. And when's that turnaround supposed to happen?' (Segment 10)

'I'll find out more tomorrow, then there'll be more I don't know.' (Segment 10)

Nick is a photojournalist who discovers that he has cancer at the very start of the film. This news, understandably, affects him greatly. He seems stunned at first, and then starts to process his new situation in different ways. One of these involves looking back over his life and reading past events, such as when he searches for how the cancer may have started, relating the information he has read about cancer to the places he has visited and activities he has undertaken. Significantly, Nick sees the world through photomontages, whereas Meryl sees it through paintings and other forms of illustration.

Nick meets Meryl early in the film and feels a connection with her at their first meeting. Despite the awkwardness of their first conversations, Nick feels drawn to Meryl, perhaps identifying the feelings of loneliness that she expresses in her painting, and relating this to his feelings of fear and isolation when he learns that he has cancer. The loneliness that each experiences is conveyed through shots that show each of them standing at the outer edges, with a gulf of space between them. This is repeated in some of the shots that feature both Nick and Andy in Segment 9.

Nick withholds his emotions for much of the film, not always managing to say what he has on his mind. The scene at his mother's, when he tries but fails to tell her that he has cancer, is indicative of the struggle that he has to tell people close to him what is troubling him. It is significant that he manages to discuss his father's death with her, as this may well be the first time they have both spoken openly of Jim's death.

Key point

The scene at the railway tracks (Segment 10) with Andy marks a turning-point for Nick. He has already told Meryl that he has cancer, but it is not until he sees Andy, and becomes angry and upset by Andy's stupid death-defying act on the tracks, that he lets out his fear and frustration about his own condition and about his fight with Meryl. This may also signify a point at which he can finally start to grieve deeply for his father.

Andy

Key quotes

'Did you do this on purpose?' (Segment 2)

'Ever got anyone pregnant?' (Segment 6)

'Anna, relationships just don't work out when they start like this.' (Segment 10)

Andy is a journalist who works at the same newspaper, *The Southern Mail*, as Nick and Phil. He is separated or divorced from Cathy, with whom he has two primary school–aged children, Maddy and Oliver. He has been in a relationship with Anna, who contacts him to tell him that she is pregnant with their baby.

Andy is a voluble and volatile character whose relationships with other people are structured through argument and acrimony. He is articulate and his profession is communication but, significantly, he does not always communicate effectively with those around him. He is brusque and clumsy, which we see when he falls over theatregoers as he exits *Macbeth*, and when he trips over prams at the cricket.

Andy's behaviour often seems to be characterised by regret and anger. He does not live in the moment, nor is he open to the possibilities contained within the moment. He does not want to contemplate having another baby because he regrets the way his previous relationship turned out. Rather, he seems stuck in a negative frame of mind, and is unhappy. The negative view he has of the world is exemplified by his campaign to show that many deaths are in fact male suicides. This unhappiness reaches its climax when he stands on the train track as the train approaches, tempting fate, as though he wants to test himself on the matter of whether to live or die. After this incident, Andy makes a decision to go to Anna, for the first time in the film.

Andy's apartment is an external indicator of his inner life. It is a mess, disorganised and entirely structured around work. It is obviously the domain of a single, working man. Pictures of car crashes on the wall show his interest in violent death.

Key point

Some long shots in the theatre foyer show Andy all alone in front of a big glass window at night, reinforcing his loneliness after leaving *Macbeth*.

Julia

Key quote

'It wasn't your fault.' (Segment 11)

Julia is the bereaved partner of Rob. She is central to the film, even though she only speaks one line of dialogue in the entire film. Julia serves as a barometer for the other characters who are also coming to terms with big issues. She works through the different stages of grief over the three days, from shock, numbness and being still, through to taking action when she builds the memorial, and to healing when the train driver visits. Normally grief takes much longer to work through; the film shows a condensed version of the process.

Key point

Julia is often filmed from a medium distance, through doorways and window frames – from a position outside the room she is in. This keeps the viewer distant from her, unable to share her grief.

Julia's grief is so personal that it is hard for anyone else to access and share. This is shown not only by the camera techniques, but also by the fact that although other people are with her, they are shadowy, and do not appear to offer her much comfort. She is not receiving any close, personal comfort from the family and friends who surround her.

Eventually Julia makes the rituals of grieving her own when she creates the memorial. Prior to this, she has had to experience her grief through rituals imposed from outside: selecting a coffin and writing a death notice.

Anna

Key quotes

'Did you see that look on the girl's face? And you wrote that maybe he had killed himself.' (Segment 10)

ANNA: You think everyone's got an agenda.
ANDY: And they don't?
ANNA: No. Things just happen. (Segment 10)

Anna works as a nurse and lives in a share household. When we meet her, we immediately learn that she is pregnant to Andy, with whom she has had a casual relationship. Anna does not appear to know what she wants when she first confronts Andy, and her body language and speech reflect this indecision.

Anna has an unusual proposal for Andy: that he look after the baby and that she pay maintenance. Note that she always uses inclusive language such as 'we won't have to abort' to emphasise that the responsibility is as much Andy's as hers. Anna is as undecided as Andy about the baby's future. It is only in the final photomontage that it is suggested that they have had the baby after all.

When Anna says to Andy that not everyone has an agenda and that 'things just happen', she is showing him an alternative way of understanding life. She says that he is as much to blame as she is, if he wants to think in terms of blame. In fact, she feels that it may not be relevant to think of the pregnancy in these terms.

Key point

Anna starts to say 'I didn't want …' then changes it to 'I don't want a baby' (Segment 2). This is an indicator that, at times, language gives away what people really think.

Cathy

Key quotes

'How can you write stuff like that?' (Segment 7)

'What's the matter with you – you didn't even want kids, and now you want to top yourself.' (Segment 7)

Cathy is the former partner of Andy, with whom she has two children. She is quite nervy and tense, often doing several things at once, such as talking to Andy on the phone while cooking and checking her daughter's television viewing. She obviously has to do the bulk of caring for the children and she doubts Andy's capacity to look after them properly, which is shown by all the instructions she gives him when he collects them from her on Sunday.

Cathy and Andy obviously have a relationship where they argue quickly and wind each other up, although it still seems to have a basis of goodwill, despite the bickering. Their continued closeness is shown by the fact that when she calls him up, they jump straight into a conversation as though they never left off the previous one. Cathy is one of the most grounded characters in the film: her childminding responsibilities anchor her in the present moment.

Q How does Cathy's reality contrast with that of Meryl, who has lots of time and space to dream and imagine?

Phil

Key quotes

'This is not about you, Andy.' (Segment 4)

'I mean, I think – apparently – it's good to stay up, and optimistic.' (Segment 6)

Phil is the newspaper editor at *The Southern Mail*. When Nick breaks the news of his cancer, Phil does not know how to react, then berates himself for his clumsiness. We can see this in the way that he reflects over what Nick has told him in Segment 1, as Nick leaves his office and makes his way back to his desk. Phil looks up at Nick again but quickly averts his gaze when Nick looks at him. In later scenes, such as at the cricket, Phil tries to empathise with Nick but again fails. Instead, he rolls out stereotypical platitudes for cancer sufferers.

We can see that Nick's news has affected Phil, because he gives up smoking, and appears to make an effort to spend more time with his family. Phil has obviously been a hardworking man, who has spent a lot of time at the office – he cannot even remember how old his daughter is. However, his thoughtful glances at the children's clothes on the line and at the party scenes suggest that he is reassessing their importance in his life.

Nick's mother, Joan

Key quote

> 'It doesn't matter how he died. Your father's death was not the sum of his life. It doesn't matter how life ends, it matters how it was. I couldn't give him my way of coping and you couldn't give him yours. Everybody has to find a way to face their own death, and life.' (Segment 10)

Nick's mother, Joan, lives alone since the death of Jim approximately a year ago. She has a healthier approach towards the death than Nick, and she has an important discussion with Nick about Jim's death in Segment 10, in which she tries to show Nick how to think about the death in a more productive way. It may well be the first open and frank discussion that they have had on this topic. Joan appears pragmatic and sensible, such as when she tells Nick that it was true that it was a problem having to make special food for Jim when he was ill. Yet she is also kind-hearted, welcoming Meryl to lunch and smiling when she sees the rescue of a child on the news.

Train driver

Key quote

> 'I'm the train driver.' (Segment 11)

The train driver only says a handful of words in the film, when he presents the card of condolences to Julia. Apart from this, all his emotion is expressed through body language. It is clear from his drooping stance and look of frustration that he has taken the death very hard and is working through it in his own time. By Sunday he manages to reconcile with his son, and makes a connection with Julia in a gesture that helps heal the pain for both of them.

The train driver's grief becomes enmeshed with his attitude towards his teenage son. We can see the problematic relationship that he has with his son through his disapproving glances towards the washing line full of gloomy black t-shirts covered in skulls, and through his almost aggressive stares at his son in earlier scenes. In Segment 10, however, when the son brings him a beer as a conciliatory gesture, the train driver decides to reciprocate, offering his son a glass.

Key point

The long shot of the two of them sitting at each end of the bench when the son brings his dad a drink of beer makes them look alone in the large expanse of backyard.

Nick's father, Jim

Key quote

'I'm liking the idea of an afterlife.' (Segment 6)

Nick's father, Jim, has died before the story commences, but we see him through Nick's flashbacks. Jim's appearances show that Nick is revisiting memories of his father's death, which have undoubtedly been triggered by his diagnosis of cancer.

Minor characters

Train driver's son

When we see the first encounter between the son and father, the son is covertly reading the newspaper about the accident but hides this from his father. It is clear that they are not communicating well: the father looks at the son as though he is trying, but failing, to understand him. In Segment 10, the son changes his goth-punk clothes for neat casual attire and flattens his spiky hair in an effort to please his father. The two start to reconcile at this point, and although we see the son try, but fail, to say something, we realise that the process of reconciliation is underway.

Key point

Segment 7 also hints at a start of reconciliation when the change in key of the music sounds a positive note, as though something has passed between the son and father. Pay attention to how non-diegetic elements such as music shape our understanding of characters.

Linda

Key quote

'And then you think, 'fantastic!' until you realise of course that is, actually, someone.' (Segment 5)

Meryl's friend Linda is talking about the fright she received that day, because of a mix-up regarding the results of medical tests she has had. She was told that she would have to have her labour induced, and was then told that the results were someone else's. Despite being relieved, Linda's experience raises the important point that one person's rejoicing can be another's suffering.

Doctor

Key quote

'Look, I really don't think there's any point in speculating in that sort of way.' (Segment 1)

When the doctor tells Nick that he has cancer, he talks to Nick with his back to him, saying that he doesn't want to speculate on what the diagnosis means. His body language makes Nick feel uncomfortable as it suggests that he is avoiding telling Nick the whole truth about his condition.

Emily

Key quote

'I just think she looks really pretty and I just think it's sad.' (Segment 8)

Emily is Anna's housemate and, like Anna, also a nurse. When the party of friends discusses Julia's picture, Emily has a very basic opinion of the matter, and she does not feel the need to analyse the situation more, unlike her friends.

Miriam

Phil's wife, Miriam, looks after their children and is very busy with day-to-day arrangements, much like Cathy, with whom she is friends. On Saturday she writes down a shopping list for the party on the newspaper, next to the photo of Julia, showing the juxtaposition of her normal family life with Julia's tragedy.

Jasmine

Phil and Miriam's daughter Jasmine is having her tenth birthday and party on the Sunday. Although she is only young, she already recognises and mocks her dad's inability to remember her age and the date of her birthday. However, she is delighted when he gives her a special birthday present of a cricket bat.

Oliver and Maddy

Oliver and Maddy are Andy and Cathy's two primary school–aged children. They are pleased to see their dad even though he takes them to an art gallery so that they can learn something.

Relationships between characters

Attraction

The differences between some characters seem to be what attracts them to one another. For example, Andy and Anna are very different: Anna is calm whereas Andy is volatile, and Anna sees possibilities where Andy just sees problems. Nick and Meryl have a number of misunderstandings when they first meet. They are similar in some respects – for example, both of their professions involve representing the world through visual media. However, their experiences of the world are still quite different: Nick sees the world through the realistic photographic images and film, whereas Meryl sees it through animation, which involves fantasy and imagination.

Meryl's attraction to themes of death is shown in her paintings of giant sharks and lone swimmers. She was already working on these paintings before her father's death. Her interest in death may be what helps her connect with Nick. Indeed, both realise that they have been 'seeing' death everywhere.

Parallel stories

The intertwining and interrelationship of all the characters' lives is one of the major themes of the film, and it is conveyed through the narrative structure. Julia's story is an illustration of the grief that the different characters feel: Nick in relation to his father and his own mortality, Meryl for her father and Anna for the potential death of her unborn child.

THEMES, IDEAS & VALUES

Death

Key quote

JOAN: It doesn't matter how life ends, it matters how it was. (Segment 10)

Look Both Ways approaches this vast theme in a variety of ways. The film's narrative is structured by death. It introduces the film in the form of Meryl's father's passing and in the news of the Arnow Hill accident. It is a possibility for Nick when we hear of his cancer diagnosis, and Rob is killed on the train tracks as Meryl walks home. All this occurs in the opening scenes of the film. This presence of death spurs the characters on to ask questions about its significance in their lives. It is often in relation to death that characters ask meaningful questions about life. For example, it is through Nick's discussion with Joan of his father's death that he comes to a realisation of a different way of viewing his own life, when Joan suggests that we should not define a life by the fact that it ends in death.

Joan's message that death is not the sum of a life is interpreted by stylistic elements of the film that show lives as constructed from myriads of moments, all of them valid and meaningful. The final photomontage of the film is a good example of how the film promotes the idea that life is a series of moments: some tragic, many ordinary, and all of them contributors to the life story of an individual.

The highs and lows of life

The film also promotes the theme that life contains highs and lows, and that we must open ourselves to this. Life goes on, even after tragedy and disaster strike. The narrative structure of *Look Both Ways* illustrates this by showing that at the same time that people's lives are torn apart by grief, the world continues to turn. For example, while Julia suffers in her bubble of numbness, Miriam writes a shopping list for her daughter's party. When grief subsides, characters such as Julia are shown to emerge from their bubble and re-engage with life. Yet the lows are not a part of life to be avoided; instead, they go hand-in-hand with the highs. It is by living through both life's tragedies and joys that we become fully human. As the photomontage at the film's end shows, Nick and Meryl will continue to have high and low moments, from Nick having treatment for his cancer to Meryl exhibiting her art. The film advocates a philosophy of acceptance of life and of not being afraid of what it may bring.

Tragedy is only one part of life

Tragedies occur and they have a serious impact on those involved when they do. However, they are only one facet of life. Sometimes, even at the heart of a tragic event there is a glimmer of hope, as illustrated by the discovery of a child alive in the Arnow Hill train wreckage.

The film emphasises the fact that even in the face of tragedy and the suffering of those involved that life goes on, in all its ordinariness. The man in the park, who jokes to Nick about his argument with Meryl in Segment 10, prevents the two characters from taking themselves too seriously. The film will not allow any one character's suffering to eclipse that of the others – it is always in perspective.

The film also raises the idea that, sometimes, other people's suffering isn't that important to us, particularly when we are constantly bombarded by the media with images of extreme suffering. It is impossible to take on the burden of the suffering of the whole world, because it would render life unliveable.

The big picture versus subjective experience

Look Both Ways frequently emphasises the fact that our personal tragedies and happy events always occur in the context of many other people's life events. It shows that we should maintain perspective and not think that our own situation is all that matters, even though it may feel like that at times. Its narrative structure, in which a number of different lives are all shown at the same time, enables us to compare characters' situations and to see that what may appear to one character as a tragedy is in fact not that serious when compared to other people's circumstances. For example, Meryl has many fears and paranoid worries about her life, yet when compared to Nick's cancer diagnosis or Julia's bereavement, we can put these worries into perspective.

Key point

The way that some shots are filmed reinforces this message that we all exist in a larger picture. In Segment 10, where Meryl and Nick have their confrontation in front of a large mural-covered wall, several shots show them as small in comparison to this huge wall. This camera technique humbles the characters.

Overcoming fear and pessimism

The film argues that we should engage with the moment instead of stopping ourselves from participating in life out of fear or pessimism. It shows that too much caution can handicap our personal development and growth. Andy and Meryl are examples of characters who restrict themselves when they give in to their fears and prejudices, and end up hurting themselves. It is only once they take the step to move towards other people and change their world views that they grow and develop as characters.

Meryl is the best example of this. We realise at the start that she would like to be in a relationship, when she discusses her life with both her sister and with Linda. However, Meryl's fear of the unknown means that she does not see the possibilities around her. In her initial encounters with Nick she is suspicious, asking him first if he is following her, and then, when he encounters her putting the papers out, asking if he wants anything. Even after they have slept together, she is reluctant to give him her phone number. Each time, Nick persists and takes the most of each opportunity to further their relationship. Although he too feels fear, he makes an effort to move beyond it.

Key point

The title of the film has special significance for understanding the film. One interpretation is that it emphasises the cautiousness that can stop us from living in the moment. Literally, 'look both ways' functions as a warning when crossing train tracks – a warning that could save a life. Metaphorically, 'look both ways' is a reminder that we should open our minds to the possibilities that are always with us but that we often ignore: the possibilities of terminal illness, of sudden death, of love surging forth, of pregnancy. It is a reminder that we should not take things for granted.

The title can also be seen as an instruction to avoid looking at life from just one perspective. The characters in the film come to terms with their personal perspectives and gain a broader view of life by looking at it in a another way. For example, Meryl gets over her obsession with death and embraces a relationship with Nick. Andy stops looking for hidden agendas, and takes responsibility for Anna's unborn child.

Q Can you think of any other interpretations of the title of the film?

Communication

Effective versus ineffective communication

Some of the characters in the film have to work hard at communicating verbally, such as Nick, who does not always manage to get the words out that he wants to say. Two significant examples of this both involve him trying to tell Meryl, and then his mother, that he has cancer. However, having the ability to express oneself in words does not necessarily mean that communication is easier. Andy is a good example of someone who is very articulate in both speech and writing, but who still manages to have many misunderstandings and arguments, perhaps because of his rage and his belief that there is always a hidden agenda. His politicisation of everyday events and attitudes clouds his perception.

Nick and Meryl illustrate the difficulty of communicating through words alone. They have some particularly awkward conversations, peppered with misunderstandings, as this quote shows.

> MERYL: Well, it was nice to see you again. Probably see you tomorrow.
> NICK: Sorry?
> MERYL: You know, it's like when you buy a car and then you see them everywhere all the time. (Segment 5)

Meryl is obviously thinking along totally different lines to Nick in this conversation.

Non-verbal communication

Notice that one of the central figures, Julia, speaks only one sentence in the entire film, when the train driver hands her a card. This shows that grief does not need words to be communicated, and also highlights the importance of the gesture made by the train driver, acknowledging his sense of responsibility for Rob's death. Julia manages to convey her grief throughout the entire film through her physical gestures and facial expressions.

The train driver's relationship with his son is also expressed elegantly through their non-verbal interactions. It is evident that the train driver feels anger towards his son because of his son's lifestyle. This is conveyed through the look that the train driver directs at his son's black t-shirts on the line, and through his expression when his son returns early on Saturday morning. His son acts sheepishly, sensing his father's disapproval. Nevertheless, this does not prevent him from reaching out again to his father, bringing him a beer on Sunday. None of this needs to be put into words; viewers understand all these nuances just through watching the actors.

The interconnectedness of people's lives

Many lives intertwine over this long weekend, in different ways: sad, joyful, poignant, reflective, troubled. This interconnection is summed up and reaches its most intense point when the train driver speaks to the widow. Tragedy is the impetus for these different connections, yet out of tragedy also comes the prospect for new and newly rediscovered relationships.

This theme of interconnectedness is not only reinforced through the relationships that develop between characters, and the apparently random pathways that lead them past one another, such as when Meryl encounters Maddy in the pool, and worries that she is drowning, but also through the shared events that we see them experiencing. All characters handle the newspaper with Julia's photo on the front at some point, although while some are interested in the photo, others, such as Cathy, are more interested in Andy's article.

Music also links characters who are in different scenes, as does the Arnow Hill incident, incessantly appearing on television screens in different characters' homes. The end-of-scene markers of the birds in the sky remind us that all these characters live under the same sky.

Personal perspective

This is shown most clearly through Meryl's imaginings of doom and bad fates befalling her, such as being swallowed up by the sea, eaten by sharks or crushed by falling trains. This shows a negative or self-defeating outlook. Similarly, once Nick has been diagnosed with cancer, he starts seeing cancer everywhere, and viewing others through the framework of illness, such as when he has the vision of the aneurysm in Andy's brain. Nick also rereads his life from the perspective of his illness, such as in the sequence where he revisits in his mind his exposure to the nuclear power plant and other toxic sites that may have triggered the disease.

The impact of media representations

The fact that Nick and Andy work for a newspaper gives us insight into how the media decides on the relative weighting given to different events. In this case, Phil decides to place the photo of Julia on the front page because he wants to help Nick remain optimistic.

The fact that an item is shown in the media does not necessarily validate it, or make it more important than things that do not appear there. Meryl's comment about why the story of her father's death is not in the paper reinforces this.

Individuals read media texts differently depending on the circumstances, such as what's happening in their personal life, their state of mind, their relationship with those represented in the media text, their knowledge of any issues under discussion, etc. This is brilliantly demonstrated in *Look Both Ways* by different characters' reactions to *The Southern Mail*'s front page story, reporting on the accident at the tracks:

- Julia is very distressed by Andy's story, probably because it theorises that her partner, Rob, actually killed himself.
- Meryl finds the photo, plus related coverage of the Arnow Hill train crash and other bad news, so overwhelming that she physically removes the paper from her studio, throwing it in the recycling.
- Cathy does not even notice the photo, but rather turns straight to Andy's article. She is more concerned with trying to find personal comments that relate to her than about Julia's story.
- Anna and Emily's friends mock the photo, analysing it from a critical perspective that sees it as yet another media ploy to grab readers' attention by using a pretty girl and shock value.
- Linda comments, 'I like her hair' (Segment 5), which is a superficial reaction to another person's tragedy.
- Miriam completely ignores the story – she uses the edge of the paper to write a shopping list for Jasmine's party.

Philosophical issues

The film can be read as a celebration of life. Although tragedy happens, ultimately those characters who experience it are shown as growing from the experience. The film offers an optimistic view of life and of relationships between people. It shows Nick and Meryl as better off for having met one another, and that Nick was right to pursue the opportunities offered by his chance meeting with Meryl. It also encourages the view that as humans, we are not here on earth for a long time, but that this is not something to be afraid of. These attitudes share elements with both existentialist philosophy and with Buddhist belief – see the Background & context section for further discussion of these ideas. Joan articulates this most clearly when she says to Nick that what matters most is how life is lived, not how death occurs.

Fate versus random events

The film presents different ways of understanding life. One is through a concept of fate or synchronicity (see below). Another sees life as open to random events. This is the view presented by Anna in Segment 10 when she says to Andy that 'things just happen'. *Look Both Ways* does not present these views as mutually exclusive; rather, it gives viewers an insight into both of them and then lets them make up their minds as to how they wish to read the film overall.

Early in the film, Meryl states that 'maybe it was meant to be' when she discusses Rob's accidental death with Nick (Segment 2). What she means is that maybe the death was not such a bad thing after all, that perhaps Rob was a person who was potentially a danger to society. She is trying to find a way to rationalise the death and make it unimportant, perhaps to try and protect herself from the awfulness of it.

However, Meryl realises straight away that the passive acceptance of fate denies people, and particularly those in poverty and misery, the ability to change their lives through positive action. The animation of malnourished African children shows her realisation of the clumsiness of her comments. Meryl realises that her comment, when taken to its logical extreme, is immensely arrogant and ignores the causes of other people's suffering.

Key point

Significantly, at the end of the film, Meryl realises that her comment that 'maybe it was meant to be' has come back on her. Sitting in the rain, Meryl laughs when a car splashes yet more water on her, and we see an animation of the African children laughing at her. Meryl has a sufficiently open mind to see that her beliefs are just as applicable to her own situation as to that of others. See the Different interpretations section for further discussion of this theme.

Synchronicity

Segment 8 is entitled 'Synchronicities'. 'Synchronicity' refers to a belief that mind and matter are connected, and that coincidental events can happen in a way that is meaningful to the person experiencing them. An example might be thinking of a person and then running into them on the street. The phenomenon of synchronicity can be used to argue that there is an underlying order in the universe and that there is some rational force underlying random events.

If we read *Look Both Ways* from a perspective that believes in synchronicity, we will think that Meryl and Nick's meeting at the train accident scene and then subsequent meetings are not accidental, but that they are in fact part of a deeper pattern. Interpreted in this way, synchronicity is similar to a belief in fate. Segment 8, shows examples of synchronicity when Andy speaks out loud of his regret over having had sex with Anna at the same time as Nick and Meryl are just starting to make love in another part of town, and as Anna reflects on her state of pregnancy.

In a wider sense of the term, Segment 8 shows that different characters are all reflecting on their personal issues at the same time. A number of them look at the moon or stand in the moonlight as they think about their problems. The whole evening is a reflective one for all the characters. The whole film suggests that these characters' lives are linked, because they all experience significant personal events at the same time. This in turn can generate a feeling of hope because it maintains that things happen for a reason, which ultimately is more comforting for many people than the idea that things happen totally randomly and for no reason. Synchronicity offers an explanation for events that would otherwise appear meaningless.

Religious understanding and the existence of God

Religion provides an important means of understanding the world for many people, particularly when they are confronted with the great certainties of life, such as birth, suffering and death. Just like psychology and politics, religion offers a framework for making sense of events, and through this it brings comfort because it enables people to find meaning in what happens to them. The film shows Jim searching for understanding through religion once he has received his cancer diagnosis. He jokes to Nick that he is trying different religions, presumably to see what comfort and support they can offer as he faces his impending death. When Nick remembers this, he then questions Andy about the existence of God, suggesting that he, in turn, is reflecting on the use of religion to face his own mortality. The prominent role that religion plays in organising the rituals of death is also shown in the photomontage in Segment 11, showing the different ways in which various religions mark the passing of a life, from floral wreaths and crucifixes through to shrines with candles and pictures of holy figures.

The film does not take any particular stance on the issue of whether there is a god or not. It raises the matter during the cricket scene (Segment 6) through the character of Nick. Andy is a resolute non-believer in any god, saying that it is all a 'crock'. Andy is taking a literal stance that does not account for faith when he tries to make the idea of a god, who is concerned with the small details of people's lives, sound implausible.

Gender roles

Some of the characters reinforce stereotypical patterns of gendered behaviour, while others actively challenge them. Nick's pursuit of Meryl and the way that he seizes opportunities to further their relationship may be read as typical gender-conditioned behaviour, where the male is the one actively pursuing the more passive female. In this respect neither Meryl nor Nick challenges these stereotypical social norms.

However, Anna actively challenges these norms when she suggests to Andy that he can have the baby to look after and she will travel and pay maintenance. As Andy has apparently suggested earlier that he would like to work from home, Anna sees this lifestyle change as compatible with their prospective new situation.

The roles that people assume indicate their value systems. Anna feels strongly that parenting is a shared responsibility, with each partner contributing equally. She is not prepared to assume the stereotypically female role of primary caregiver.

The configuration of Andy and Cathy's family after the divorce suggests that they have subscribed to a more traditional set of values, where the woman gets the house, car and the children, and the man sees the children on weekends.

The significance of place

Look Both Ways pays close attention to people's surroundings and habitats. It seems to be saying that we can find out about people's personalities through observation of where they spend their time. The opening frames of the film show Meryl's mother's house through a series of static interior shots, like still-life paintings. We gain a sense of the person who lives there through this technique. When we encounter Meryl's studio-apartment for the first time, the camera introduces us to her space so that we can gain a sense of how she lives and works.

Places are also significant because of characters' relationships to them. Both Julia's house and the place of Rob's death are significant places that are visited throughout the course of the film by different characters. It is as though these physical locations focus the characters' anxieties about death or their own situations. The accident site where Rob is killed is the setting for one of the key scenes, when Andy defies death and Nick finally manages to tell him that he has cancer. This site is significant because of the event that happened there, but the film reminds us that its significance has to be perpetuated through memory and memorialisation.

Values

Responsibility

Andy's flirtation with suicide shows his irresponsibility, but the incident seems to make him decide to assume greater responsibility for his life. In the following scene he visits Anna, presumably to sort out their situation instead of running away from it.

Q Is it possible to attribute Andy's contemplation of suicide to genuine problems in his life?

By showing all the different characters and how their lives interrelate, the film promotes a message of responsibility. If the film were to have focused on Andy's experience and not let us into the world of Anna to the extent that it does, it may have underplayed Andy's responsibility by failing to show the consequences of his actions.

Similarly, the film shows us the train driver's burden, and by doing so, illustrates how some people take on responsibility for something even when they shouldn't. Unlike Andy and Anna, the train driver is not directly responsible for his predicament. However, his demeanour throughout the film shows how he has been burdened by the knowledge that he has killed a man. He feels this keenly and does not try to avoid it: rather, his depressed stance and crying show that he is grappling to come to terms with it.

The scene where he approaches Julia shows that he has come to terms with this knowledge, to the extent that he is prepared to face up to her and reveal his identity. Julia may not have wanted to see him, or may have blamed him, but he takes the chance, and luckily for him, the moment is a healing one. By showing the meeting between Julia and the train driver in a positive light, the film promotes the message that it is good to accept responsibility for one's actions and face up to potentially difficult situations, even when it is hard to do so.

Honesty

Honesty is linked to the value of responsibility because without being honest to themselves and to others, some of the characters would not have been able to assume responsibility for their actions. The film presents those episodes where characters manage to say what they really feel and think as rewarding moments, showing that it is better to be frank and honest than to withhold this information. Nick and Joan's angry discussion of their different attitudes towards Jim's death allows them both to better understand what the other is feeling, and allows Nick in particular to view his father's death in a more positive light.

Key point

Although Meryl and Nick's confrontation initially proves overwhelming for Meryl, who runs away, the revelations of their personal fears ultimately serve to bring them together and to let them know where they each stand in their relationship.

DIFFERENT INTERPRETATIONS

Fate, random events and human agency

The film could be read as arguing that fate governs our lives, or it could be understood as showing that random events rule them. Another view is that human beings have the power to significantly alter the course of their lives through making choices. Different characters present these different points of view about events in their lives, namely Rob's death and Anna and Andy's pregnancy.

Random events

Anna subscribes to the view that 'things just happen' (Segment 10). She believes that there is not always a logical explanation or reason behind why events occur, and this is how she understands the pregnancy. However, even though she sees the event as random and as an accident, she is still prepared to accept responsibility for the consequences, and she feels that Andy ought to do so also.

Anna does not think that the death was suicide, but a tragic accident. She is shocked to read Andy's interpretation of it and confronts him angrily, accusing him of insensitivity. Anna looks at the situation from Julia's point of view. Julia has just lost her partner, and Anna feels outraged that Andy would even consider his interpretation of the death. Anna's reading of the death as accidental fits in with her understanding that 'things just happen', whereas Andy's suicide theory belongs to his view that everyone has an agenda, and that things happen for a reason.

Fate – 'it was meant to be'

When Meryl states that 'maybe it was meant to be' (Segment 2), she raises the spectre of fate, suggesting that there was a reason behind Rob's death: that he was potentially going to commit a crime, and that therefore there is some cosmic justice governing the world. However, she also realises the fallacy of this notion, which is that it can tie people's misery and suffering into a framework in which they are seen as unavoidable and incontrovertible. It also removes the sense of empowerment we feel from believing that our choices have an impact on what happens in our lives.

Human agency

The events in *Look Both Ways* can also be looked at as being strongly influenced by human agency. Andy's obsession with hidden intrigues and personal power agendas illustrates this point. Andy is convinced that Rob's death is no accident. Right from his arrival at the accident scene he reads events in terms of suicide, questioning Meryl's assertion that he must have tripped, and checking that Nick has got his angle on the story.

Note that we never actually find out for certain how Rob died. The film implies that Andy's interpretation is wrong, but it never definitively explains what has happened.

Many of the characters take control of their lives by making decisions. For example, Nick decides to visit Meryl and they end up having sex, beginning their relationship. Meryl decides to stick by Nick and help him through his illness. Even in the face of random events, human agency is still a very powerful force.

Life as meaningful versus life as meaningless

It would be possible to read the film's statements about the meaning of life from very different perspectives. Overall, the film promotes a positive view. However, there is scope for reading it as a much darker tale than it presents itself as. Even though the director has structured the film as a romantic comedy, a viewer who was not willing to indulge the humour or the quirkiness could interpret the film as much bleaker, and could read the unrelenting focus on death and physical decline as a cold reminder of the only certainty that we ever have.

The quote from *Macbeth* that describes life as 'a tale/Told by an idiot, full of sound and fury,/Signifying nothing' (Segment 8) presents a nihilistic view of life. It is bleak because it cannot see any purpose to life beyond the fact that we exist and then we die.

The film itself seems to promote a more positive view of life, considering both tragic and joyous events as worthwhile and meaningful in themselves. Consider how these two perspectives may read the following events differently.

Event 1: Meryl and Nick's union

Interpretation – life is meaningless:

- This is a last refuge against fear and loneliness and an attempt to salvage something from the depressing events in their lives.
- The final photomontage shows that nothing is certain: Nick still has a troubled future ahead of him as he grapples with his illness.

Interpretation – life is meaningful:

- This is the start of a rewarding new relationship that will take them into a hopeful future. Although their life together is by no means guaranteed, every moment that passes has its own worth.
- The final photomontage presents future moments as something worth celebrating.

Event 2: Andy's quasi-suicide attempt

Interpretation – life is meaningless:

- This is Andy's last authentic action in the face of a world that does not care whether he lives or dies; a final attempt to look the ultimate truth of death in the face.
- Andy's eventual move towards Anna signals a failure to confront the meaning of life.

Interpretation – life is meaningful:

- This is an irresponsible act and an attempt to escape the consequences of his sexual relationship with Anna.
- Andy's eventual acceptance of the situation and his move towards Anna is shown in a positive light as it occurs with all the other moments of reconciliation within the film.

QUESTIONS & ANSWERS

Essay topics

1 'Andy is an irresponsible character who is reluctant to admit to his mistakes.' Discuss.

2 'Nick and Meryl come together only out of their fears of loneliness and death.' Discuss.

3 'Meryl's fears are the paranoid imaginings of a woman who has too much time on her hands.'
Compare Meryl's experience with that of other characters in *Look Both Ways*.

4 'The animation and photomontages mean that we learn about Nick and Meryl more than other characters in the film.' Discuss.

5 'Julia and the train driver only have small speaking parts; however, their roles are crucial to our understanding of the other characters.' Discuss.

6 'The film demonstrates that death is a universal human experience.' Discuss.

7 'This text shows that, ultimately, we must all face the consequences of our actions.' Discuss.

8 '*Look Both Ways* shows that a fear of death can prevent people from living fully.' Discuss.

9 'Although speaking the truth can be difficult, the text shows that people should be honest with one another.' Discuss.

10 '*Look Both Ways* challenges the norms of standard male–female relationships.' Do you agree?

Analysing a sample topic

'The film demonstrates that death is a universal human experience.' Discuss.

- Analyse the contention and ask whether there are any other issues raised by it that you need to consider. Do you agree with it totally, partially or not at all? Remember that this statement is an assertion that can be challenged.
- In this case, you could agree that the film shows the universality of death. However, you would also want to argue that, at the same time, people's responses are highly individualised, and that different cultures have developed their own rituals for grieving. You should also define a context for 'death': i.e. are you going to discuss people's reactions to others' deaths, such as mourning, or their reaction to their own prospective death?
- Write down a series of relevant points from the text, using your in-depth knowledge of the characters and themes. It may include the following:
  - Deaths in the film: Nick's father, Meryl's father, the death of many in the Arnow Hill accident, Rob's death, Nick's potential death.
  - Responses to death: Meryl's shock and numbness, Nick's self-reflection, Julia's move through the stages of grief, the train driver's reaction, more flippant reactions from Linda and the dinner party guests, Andy's suicide theory.
  - Rituals surrounding death: mainly seen through Julia, though not exclusively – funerals (choice of coffin), sympathy cards, newspaper notices. Memorials – a floral wreath, Meryl's 'art' piece, Julia's construction.
- Plan the argument: formulate your stance on the contention that the topic proposes. Organise your material into main topic headings that advance your stance. Outline the scope of the essay.

- For example: 'The film demonstrates that, although death is a universal human experience, people's responses to it are highly individualised.'
    - Topic 1: Outline the deaths in the film. How does the film characterise death as a universal part of human experience?
    - Topic 2: Individualised responses – Meryl's and Julia's memorials. Show how these link to social and cultural ritual.

Sample introduction

> The film demonstrates that, although death is a universal human experience, people's responses to it are highly individualised. Through the connection it forges between the disastrous Arnow Hill train wreck and the tragedy of Rob's death, *Look Both Ways* shows that the loss of another human being is something that we must all encounter at some point. However, how people react to death is mediated by their personal situation, their social circumstances and the culturally prescribed rituals that they are encouraged to engage with.

- The conclusion should return to the main points canvassed in the introduction, with an added statement about how the essay has provided insight into them. It should briefly recap the journey that the essay has taken the reader on.

SAMPLE ANSWER

'The animation and photomontages mean that we learn more about Nick and Meryl than other characters in the film.' Discuss.

The use of visual inserts within the main film narrative enables *Look Both Ways* to convey a great range of complexity and insight into characters and to expand on what a more standard film would have shown. Both Nick's and Meryl's visions enable us to access their hidden fears and preoccupations in a direct and immediate way. However, other methods, such as an acting style that relies on physical expression rather than dialogue, also allow us to understand the subtleties of other characters' feelings and situations.

The use of the animations to show viewers Meryl's fears is an innovative and original means of fleshing out a film character. The fact that they are painted and drawn illustrations not only shows us the kind of work that Meryl does, but also creates a lyrical and poetic feel to the film that makes Meryl's loneliness and anxiety more poignant. Nick's photomontages also complement the picture we have of him, as we know that he is a professional photographer. Their use underlines the fact that Nick understands the world through images, rather than through words. This is significant because, as we see, Nick finds it hard to express himself in speech. Montages, such as the succession of funeral wreaths in the final scene, let us into Nick's memory and allow us to speed along with his thoughts much more immediately than a voice-over would, for example.

Although the animations and graphic sequences are a key feature of this film, there is another significant mode through which information is conveyed, which is that of physical expression. Julia's grief, the despondency of the train driver and the train driver's son's yearning to reach out to his father are all conveyed in striking detail by these characters, who either say nothing or only a sentence each. Julia in particular occupies a central place in the film, with her behaviour often acting as a distillation of other characters' grief and turmoil. Through their actions and gestures, we see how these characters grow and develop over the course of the film, moving from states of shock and despair to an acceptance of the fates that have befallen them.

Yet another way that viewers learn about the characters in the film is through verbal expression. Aside from the obvious way in which dialogue reveals characters' thoughts and emotions, it is also their hesitancies and verbal mistakes that make significant points. When Anna changes 'I didn't want …' to 'I don't want a baby', we learn that she may have changed her mind about wanting to have the baby. Phil's repeated clumsy comments, such as 'I mean, I think, it's good to stay up', betray his desire to pass on a positive message that is limited by his lack of practical understanding about the experience of cancer sufferers.

We do gain significant insight into Nick and Meryl through the extra filmic devices that show their subjective experiences. However, given that Nick and Meryl are the two main protagonists, we can expect that the film's focus will remain on them for much of the time. Although most of the other characters are only supports for these two, the film nevertheless manages to provide us with a rich understanding of their hopes, fears and challenges, creating a rich sense of a very human community.

REFERENCES & READING

Text

Look Both Ways 2004, dir. Sarah Watt, Footprint Films/Dendy Films. Starring William McInnes, Justine Clarke and Anthony Hayes.

Newspaper articles

Byrnes, Paul 2005, Review of *Look Both Ways*, *Sydney Morning Herald*, 20 August, http://www.smh.com.au/news/reviews/look-both-ways/2005/08/19/1123958224257.html?oneclick=true

Hawker, Philippa 2005, 'Different Ways of Looking', *The Age*, 6 August, http://www.theage.com.au/news/film/different-ways-of-looking/2005/08/06/1123125836993.html

Ryan, Tom 2005, Review of *Look Both Ways*, *The Age*, 14 August, http://www.theage.com.au/news/reviews/look-both-ways/2005/08/11/1123353442402.html

Film

Living With Happiness 2001, dir. Sarah Watt, Sarah Watt Productions.